Basic
Financial Skills
for the
Public Sector

Basic
Financial Skills
for the
Public Sector

Essential Skills for the Public Sector

Jennifer Bean 21/7/06

Lascelles Hussey

HB
PUBLICATIONS

HB Publications
(Incorporated as Givegood Limited)

Published by

HB Publications
London, England

British Library Cataloguing in Publication Data

ISBN 1 899448 09 8

Printed and bound in England by Short Run Press Ltd.

Contents

Chapter 1

INTRODUCTION

Public sector managers will increasingly find finance to be an important part of their role, and a basic understanding of finance is now essential to the delivery of Best Value services.

This book seeks to provide the public sector manager with basic skills often overlooked in other finance texts. It is usually assumed that managers know how to use a calculator, and that they are familiar with certain basic calculations such as percentages. There is also an assumption that a manager is able to present information in a numerical format, and can undertake data analysis in order to make management decisions that may have financial implications. This book does not make these assumptions. It gives a quick overview of the underpinning knowledge needed to use and manipulate figures effectively. The key areas covered show the reader how to undertake basic calculations; use statistics; make use of spreadsheets; appraise projects; and present financial information.

Basic Financial Skills for the Public Sector, has been designed such that it can be used for reference and act as an important part of a manager's own personal development. The book contains exercises that encourage the reader to focus on the issues covered therein. Suggested solutions for the exercises are provided in the final section of the text.

This is a practical book, which seeks to demonstrate how the skills and techniques covered can be applied to a public sector environment, and enables the reader to use the newly developed skills in the workplace with confidence.

Chapter 2

BASIC CALCULATIONS

Using Your Calculator

In order to undertake simple financial calculations, it is necessary to understand how to use a calculator. Shown below is a diagram of the most common and basic calculator functions:

M+	M-	MR	MC	x
%	7	8	9	÷
+/−	4	5	6	−
C	1	2	3	+
AC	0	.	=	

The function keys shown above are described as follows:

Symbol	Function	Symbol	Function
+	Addition	M+	Memory plus: adds numbers to the total figure in the memory
−	Subtraction	M-	Memory minus: subtracts numbers from the total figure in the memory
x	Multiplication	MR	Memory recall: shows the figure being held in the memory
÷	Division	MC	Memory clear: clears the memory to zero

Symbol	Function	Symbol	Function
=	Equals sign: when pressed gives the outcome of all the mathematical functions undertaken to that point	+/-	Plus to Minus: changes a positive number into a negative number or vice versa.
C	Clear: clears the number currently entered on the calculator without clearing the function being undertaken. For example, if whilst adding a series of numbers an error is made, the last entry can be cleared using this key and the correct number entered and the addition continued	AC	All Cancel: pressing this key will clear all numbers and functions
		%	Percentage: this key performs percentage calculations

These function keys are common to all calculators. An understanding of the above is all that is required for the majority of financial exercises likely to be encountered by the public sector manager.

Fractions and Percentages

Fractions and percentages are amongst the most common calculations needed for the presentation and analysis of numerical data. The public sector manager needs to be very conversant in how to calculate, and then present fractions and percentages.

Fractions show the number of parts of a whole number. For example, 10 people out of 50 is represented as a fraction of 10 over 50, where 10 represents the ***numerator*** and 50 the ***denominator***.

It is normal to show fractions in the following way:

$$\frac{10}{50}$$

This fraction is ten fiftieths. Fractions are usually shown at their lowest possible level, which is to have the numerator and denominator as near to 1 as possible. In this case, if you divide the numerator and denominator by 10 (which is the common denominator), the fraction becomes one fifth. Therefore, instead of saying ten people out of 50, we could say one fifth of people. In order to identify the common denominator, it is necessary to identify the largest number by which both the denominator and numerator can be divided.

It is common to express fractions in terms of percentages. This is particularly useful when the fraction is not one of the more commonly known fractions, but a more complex number such as 32 over 71. Percentages express the fraction in terms of parts of one hundred. In order to calculate the percentage, one must undertake the division represented by the fraction. In the above example, this is 1 divided by 5, which equals 0.2. This is then multiplied by 100 to give 20, (20 per cent) which represents 20 parts of 100.

Percentages are easily calculated with the aid of a calculator by following these steps:

Enter the numerator	*e.g.*	*1*
Press divide		*÷*
Enter the denominator	*e.g.*	*5*
Press percentage		*%*

The calculator will then display the result as 20 which represents 20%.

We could also calculate 20% of a number, for example, 20% of 50. This is again easily performed using the calculator as follows:

Enter the number	*50*
Press multiply	*x*
Enter the percentage amount	*20*
Press percentage	*%*

The calculator will then display the result as <u>10</u>

Managers are often required to calculate the percentage increase or decrease of activities. For example, calculate the percentage increase in users of a service that has increased from 500 to 575 users. Again the following steps are undertaken:

Identify the increase in absolute terms (ie 575 - 500)	*75*
Press divide	*÷*
Enter the base figure, ie the figure from which	
we are increasing	*500*
Press percentage	*%*

The calculator will then display the result as <u>15</u> which represents a 15% increase.

If the number of users has fallen from 500 to 450, then the following steps are necessary to identify the percentage decrease:

Identify the decrease in absolute terms (ie 500 - 450)	*50*
Press divide	*÷*
Enter the base figure, ie the figure from which	
we are decreasing	*500*
Press percentage	*%*

The calculator will then display the result as <u>10</u> which represents a 10% decrease.

Percentages are a common and useful tool for any manager wishing to present information requiring:

- Comparisons year on year
- Comparisons between different activities
- Comparisons between similar activities
- Trends
- Growth rates
- Occupancy rates
- Profit margins
- Direct v Indirect Costs ......and so on

It is useful to be aware of the most common fractions and their corresponding percentages, and these are presented in the following table:

Fraction	Percentage %	Fraction	Percentage %
1/2	50.0	1/8	12.5
1/4	25.0	3/8	37.5
3/4	75.0	5/8	62.5
1/3	33.3	7/8	87.5
2/3	66.6	1/5	20.0

Calculating Budget Profiles

Many public sector managers now hold some form of budgetary responsibility which may involve them in budget preparation and monitoring. One important tool in the preparation and monitoring of budgets is "profiling". Profiling the budget allows the manager to predict and plan how a particular budget will be spent during the year. In some areas, this is crucial as the budget may be heavily affected by peaks and troughs in demand. This may arise as a result of seasonal fluctuations or planned events.

A profiled budget enables the manager to take greater control over the pattern of expenditure, and identifies large over or under spending sooner rather than later. Profiling is much more accurate than a "straight-line profile", which assumes that a budget is spent in twelve equal amounts during the year.

Profiled budgets are easily created using percentages. The manager should identify what percentage of the budget will be spent monthly, and this can then be used to allocate financial resources. For example:

A social services department provides home care services for older people. They have undertaken research into the patterns of annual expenditure in order to assist in budgetary control activities. This research shows that each year there is a significant increase in demand for services during the winter months. The average spend per client in the winter months is 50% higher than that for the rest of the year. The home care service also established that there was a continuing steady growth in demand year on year as numbers of users increase (more people are living longer). This general growth rate appears to be climbing year on year at a rate of 10%. With this information, the department is able to calculate a budget estimate for the following year using percentages.

Assuming the average spend per client is £1,000 per month for spring, summer and autumn, and the number of clients for the previous year was 500, then the spend in winter months would be £1,500 (i.e. £1,000 + 50% of £1,000) and the number of clients for the following year would be 550 (i.e. 500 +10% of 500). Assuming no inflation, the budget calculation for the following year would be:

	£
<u>*Spring, Summer & Autumn*</u>	
550 clients @ £1000 per client per month	
multiplied by 9 months	*4,950,000*
<u>*Winter*</u>	
550 clients @ £1500 per client per month	
multiplied by 3 months	*2,475,000*
Total for the year	<u>*7,425,000*</u>

The budget profile shows how the total budget should be spent over the twelve months. This would take into account the seasonal fluctuation with respect to the winter months. Based on the above example, the following table identifies the profile.

Month	Planned Expenditure (£)	Percentage of Budget (%)
April	550,000	7.4*
May	550,000	7.4
June	550,000	7.4
July	550,000	7.4
August	550,000	7.4
September	550,000	7.4
October	550,000	7.4
November	550,000	7.4
December	825,000	11.1
January	825,000	11.1
February	825,000	11.1
March	550,000	7.4
Total	**7,425,000**	**100****

* eg $\dfrac{550,000}{7,425,500} \times 100 = 7.4\%$

** rounded up

Note: The percentages are rounded to one decimal place.

It is usual to enter the budget profile onto the organisation's general ledger accounting system. However, the manager can also enter the profile onto a local accounting system be it paper based or a spreadsheet. Regardless of where the profile is used, by comparing the planned against actual monthly expenditure, the profiled budget can be used as an effective monitoring tool.

Calculating Projected Outturns

The projected outturn for any budget is an estimation of the "end of year position". This is calculated by taking into account the current position, (i.e., expenditure to date), the planned future expenditure, (e.g. the profiled budget), and any known future events. The outturn will be more accurate, if the manager develops well thought out and realistic budget expectations for the remaining months. The projected outturn can also be calculated on a purely mathematical basis using the profiled budget. This is shown in the example below:

An ambulance service has undertaken extensive research into the cost and number of monthly callouts. A clear pattern has emerged where callouts increase significantly at certain times of the year, Christmas and New Year being by far the highest, followed by April. Using this information, the management team was able to develop a profiled budget based on historic trends. Three months into the financial year, the management team have decided to review the budget and calculate a projected outturn based on the first three months' actual figures.

Month	Original Profiled Budget £'000	Monthly Profile %	Cumulative Profile %	Actual Expenditure to date £'000	Projected outturn* £'000
April	500	10	10	625	625
May	400	8	18	500	500
June	400	8	26	500	500
July	400	8	34	n/a	500
August	300	6	40	n/a	375
September	300	6	46	n/a	375
October	300	6	52	n/a	375
November	400	8	60	n/a	500
December	600	12	72	n/a	750
January	600	12	84	n/a	750
February	400	8	92	n/a	500
March	400	8	100	n/a	500
Total	5,000	100			6,250 **

---

* *The projected outturn is either the actual expenditure for the period or a projection of expenditure using the profile percentages and the actuals to date as a base.*

** *£6,250 is the total of the 3 months actual expenditure figures (which total £1,625), and the remaining 9 months projected outturn. As £1,625 represents 26% of profiled expenditure, then the outturn of £6,250 is simply* $\frac{1625}{0.26}$

The monthly projected outturns from July onwards are calculated by using the profile percentages, hence July's outturn is £6,250 x 8%, and so on for other months

---

There are other mathematical ways of projecting the outturn, these include:

- Using the actual figures and adding the remainder of the profiled budget, assuming that expenditure will revert to plan in future months
- Using the actual figures and subtracting this from the total budget, spreading the balance of the budget over the remaining months in line with the profile percentages. This results in the projected outturn equalling the original budget but with new spending targets for the remaining months.

Exercise 1

Simple Fractions and Percentages

Fractions show the number of parts of a whole number. It is common practice to reduce the fraction to the lowest possible value using a common denominator, a figure that can be divided into both the numerator and denominator.

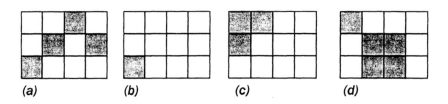

(a)   (b)   (c)   (d)

Looking at the shaded areas, state the fractions in relation to (a), (b), (c), and (d) above.

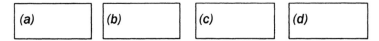

(a)   (b)   (c)   (d)

Fractions can be translated into percentages. A fraction is part of a whole and is always less than 1. To express a fraction as a percentage, we divide the numerator by the denominator and multiply by 100.

Restate the fractions in (a), (b), (c) and (d) above as percentages.

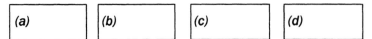

(a)   (b)   (c)   (d)

Suggested solution given on page 65.

Exercise 2

Budgets and Outturns as percentages

Using one of your key budget areas, identify your planned monthly spend and then calculate each month's spend as a percentage of this budget. Use the profile percentages to then calculate the projected outturn. (See example in this chapter for assistance.)

- Note when the actual spend for a particular month is known, this will be the outturn for that month.

Month	Profiled Budget	Budget %	Actual Expenditure	Projected Outturn	Assumptions
April					
May					
June					
July					
August					
September					
October					
November					
December					
January					
February					
March					
TOTAL		**100%**			

Chapter 3

USING STATISTICS

Importance of Statistical Information

Research often involves the collection, analysis and interpretation of numerical data, which can enable organisations to assess the effectiveness of their services and plan for the future. Research data may be collected in a way that lends itself to numerical interpretations, and hence statistics are used to analyse and then present the data.

In order to calculate a statistic, there is a need to obtain data. Data is defined as, "known facts or things used as a basis for inference or reckoning" (Concise Oxford Dictionary). Data can be gained from a variety of internal and external sources such as:

Primary research data from
- *questionnaires*
- *interviews*
- *observations*
- *experiments*
- *record keeping...* and so on

Secondary research data from
- *historical records*
- *books and journals*
- *published reports and surveys...* and so on

Statistics have many uses as illustrated in the following table:

Purpose	Example
Historical record of the facts - which may then be used for comparisons or measuring performance	In 199X we emptied 80% of refuse bins on time
Justification of an historic decision - demonstration of the impact the decision has had	As a result of the office closure we have saved 20% of overhead costs
Justification of a future decision - estimating the impact of the decision using current and expertly assessed future predictions	If we invest in a recycling plant, we will increase our recycling levels to the national average for next year, which is expected to be 10% of all household waste products
Future planning - past and current trends extrapolated to predict the future	The demand for parking permits was up by 6% last year, 5% the year before that and current levels show an expected 7% increase this year. Hence, we should plan for an 8% increase next year
Assessment of outcomes - analysing results of long term strategies and undertaking cost benefit analysis	As a result of the investment in added security, the cost of vandalism on this estate is down by 80% compared with 5 years ago
Customer relations - identifying satisfaction levels and complaint levels, and testing ideas and suggestions	We have a 95% satisfaction rating for the services currently provided, and 84% of those questioned prefer an appointment system
Marketing and presentation of information - to maximise impact, create positive images, and sell services or ideas	Of those who have taken up our special payment arrangements, 9 out of 10 people have benefited from reduced council tax bills

The usefulness of statistics tends to vary depending on:

a)   The origin of the data
b)   The sample size, and segmentation criteria
c)   The accuracy of the data
d)   The currency (how up to date is the data)

Calculating Averages - mean, median, mode

Where an activity or event has many discrete pieces of data with differing values, it is usual to identify the central tendency, or average, and refer to this when describing the data set. For example, we often refer to the following;

- The average height
- The average weight
- The average IQ
- The average journey time.....and so on

There are three measures of the central tendency which are discussed as follows:

The mean	**The arithmetic average**
The median	**The middle value**
The mode	**The most common result in a frequency data set**

The Mean

The arithmetic mean is calculated by taking the sum of a number of discrete values making up the data set, and dividing that total by the number of values in the data set.

A mathematical representation of this is shown below:

$$\frac{\sum x}{n} = \text{the arithmetic mean}$$

where

$$n = \text{number of values in a data set}$$
$$\sum x = \text{the sum of the values in a data set}$$

Calculation of the mean is illustrated in the following examples:

Example (a)

There are 21 elderly residents in the Langton residential home whose ages range between 60 and 80 years old. A list of their ages are given as follows:

| 60 | 62 | 62 | 62 | 65 | 65 | 65 | 66 | 66 | 67 | 69 | 70 | 70 | 70 | 70 | 70 | 70 | 72 | 73 | 75 | 80 |

The number of values in the data set (n) is 21
The total of the values in the data set $\sum x$ is 1429
The arithmetic mean equals 1429/21 = 68
The average age is 68 years.

Example (b)

In the case of 20 weekly paid catering staff, we have the following salary payments for one week:

	£		£
1	110	11	150
2	110	12	150
3	120	13	160
4	120	14	160
5	120	15	170
6	140	16	170
7	140	17	280
8	150	18	290
9	150	19	300
10	150	20	360

The number of values in the data set (n) is 20
The total of the values in the data set $\sum x$ is 3500
The arithmetic mean equals 3500/20 = 175
The average weekly salary is £175.

The Median

The median is defined as the central value or the middle result. In example (a) above, there were 21 Langton residents whose ages were presented in ascending order. The central value will be the value occupying the 11th position, which is the middle spot with 10 values on either side. Counting along the list, we see that age 69 is the median value.

In example (b), with 20 weekly paid staff there are two central values, the 10th and 11th. The median is taken to be half their sum, $\frac{1}{2}(150+150)$, which in this case is £150.

The Mode

The mode represents the value that occurs most in any group of values. It is possible to have two such values in which case the data is bi-modal. The mode is the value that has the highest frequency.

We can go back to the data set in example (a), and rewrite it such that we can see the frequency of each value. The frequency is denoted by the symbol f

Age	f
60	1
62	3
65	3
66	2
67	1
69	1
70	6
72	1
73	1
75	1
80	1

In this example, age 70 is the mode because it occurs 6 times, i.e. it has the highest frequency. A similar table could be drawn up for example (b), and this would show that the mode was £150.

Each of the central tendency measures have advantages and disadvantages, and the most appropriate choice will depend on the data set and the purpose of the statistic. In the case of example (a), the results of all three measures were:

Mean - 68   Median - 69   Mode - 70

There is little difference between all the central tendency measures due to the relatively even spread of ages across the 21 clients, and consequently, any of these measures could be used to represent the average. However, if a manager needed to make a decision based on the average age of clients, then the median should be utilized as that indicates the mid-point of the three averages.

In the case of example (b), the results of all these measures were:

Mean - 175   Median - 150   Mode - 150

It is clear that the arithmetic mean is quite different from the median and the mode. The reason for this is the spread of wages is quite wide, with several of the weekly wages being considerably higher than the others, causing the arithmetic mean to be skewed. In this case, the median and mode may give a truer reflection of the most common rate of weekly pay than the arithmetic mean.

It is useful for managers to be aware of the different methods for calculating a central tendency, and although the mean is the most commonly used, the median and mode may in some circumstances be more representative of the average and hence provide a better basis for decision-making.

Interpreting Statistical Data

It is well known that statistics can be presented in different ways. Therefore, whilst a set of statistics can be used to present an argument for one view point, the same set of statistics can be used to present a totally different view. This is not uncommon, especially in areas such as politics. It should be remembered that statistics should be based on factual information and it is the interpretation and presentation of the information that wins or loses the arguments. For example,

a) 9 out of 10 dog owners use "Champ" dog food
b) 10% fall in unemployment
c) 95% satisfaction rating
d) 5th in league table

It is often what is <u>not</u> said about the figures presented which reveals the slant being given to information. For example, the following questions need to be raised with respect to each of the previous statements:

a) **How big was the sample? e.g. did we speak to every dog owner in the country to identify the feeding preferences, or was the sample only 50 dog owners in a local village.**

b) **Over what period was the 10% fall in unemployment measured? e.g. 1 year or 10 years.**

c) **What type of questions were asked and on what criteria was satisfaction being measured? Again if the sample was small, the results could also be queried.**

d) **How many were in the league, 6 or 100? The answer puts the 5th place into it proper perspective.**

We can see from the above example, how the presentation of statistics affects our assessment and understanding of a particular position. All managers now require knowledge of how to understand statistics and utilise them to their advantage.

The manager may wish to interpret statistical results in a way that will help to predict the future. As the future is not certain, using statistics can help to justify a hypothesis of what is expected to happen, and hence form the basis for future planning. This is significantly better than guess work, or assuming a status quo situation in what is clearly a changing environment. Even so, statistical inferences do not produce certainties, and the manager may wish to consider the technique of "probability".

Probability

The probability of an event, is the likelihood that it is going to happen. For example, when we look at a trend, such as the aging population, statistical results show that average life expectancy has now increased to 80 years. A manager may, therefore, wish to know what is the probability that the average life expectancy will continue to increase at the same rate over the next fifty years. Calculating this type of probability will assist in allocating resources to meet the probable increase in demand for services created by an aging population.

Probabilities can be subjectively estimated or based on research data gained from actual experience, historic events or experimentation. Probabilities can be applied to all kinds of statistical information and will assist in their interpretation. The key points to understand about probabilities are as follows:

- **A probability is a number between zero and one, and represents the likelihood of something happening, e.g. when flipping a coin the probability of it landing on heads is 50%. (i.e. there is a 1 in 2 chance of it being heads)**
- **A certainty would be a probability of 1**
- **An impossibility is a probability of 0**
- **Probabilities of all the possibilities must add up to 1**

A mutually exclusive event, is one where there can only be one outcome thus excluding the possibility of alternative outcomes. In such cases, the probabilities are related to each other and when added together will total 1. For example, if there are three tenderers bidding for a contract and the probability of tenderer A winning is 60%, tenderer B winning 10%, and tenderer C winning 30%, then the probability of A or C winning is 90%. However, as only one tenderer can win the contract, the probability of more than one winning must be 0, that is, an impossibility.

An independent event is where two activities are separate from each other, that is the probability of event A happening does not affect the probability of event B happening. However, the probability of both A and B happening, is equal to the probability of A multiplied by the probability of B. For example, if the ambulance service considers the probability of being 100% occupied on Saturday night is 90%, and being 100% occupied on Sunday night is 80%, then the probability of being 100% occupied on Saturday and Sunday night is 72%, (90% x 80%).

A dependent event, is where two activities are related to each other. The outcome from event A affects the probability of event B. For example, mutually exclusive events are dependent because if event A occurs the probability of event B happening must be zero.

Set out below is an example of how using the statistical techniques described in this chapter, can assist the manager in analysing past events and planning for the future.

The manager of a small nursery with 10 staff has been monitoring sickness related absence for the last three years and has collected data for each member of staff. All staff have been with the nursery for over three years, and the manager is concerned that the expenditure on agency staff engaged to cover sickness absence seems to be increasing each year.

Number	Initials of staff member	Days Absent Year 1	Days Absent Year 2	Days Absent Year 3	Average Days over 3 years
1	HA	6	6	10	7.3
2	CD	12	10	12	11.3
3	LD	10	10	10	10.0
4	WF	10	12	14	12.0
5	GJ	6	10	12	9.3
6	JM	1	5	6	4.0
7	PP	16	15	12	14.3
8	RS	14	12	14	13.3
9	CT	10	10	12	10.7
10	TW	5	10	8	7.7
Total		90	100	110	100 *

* *rounded up*

In order to identify potential problems and plan more adequately for the future, the manager has decided to use statistics to analyse and interpret this information and undertook the following calculations:

The average number of days absence per staff member for the current year, year 3, (the mean)	110 /10 = 11 days
During the current year, year 3, the most common number of days absence taken by staff (the mode)	12 days (there are 4)
Comparison of the average number of days absence taken by staff over the last three years, with the target set for the organisation which is 8 days per annum	100/10 = 10 days over the last 3 years 2 days more than the target or 25% above the target (2/8x100)
The number of staff exceeding the sickness absence target in the most recent year	In year 3, 8 out of 10 exceeded the target of 8 days or 80% of staff (8/10 x 100)
Between years 1 & 2 and years 2 & 3, the total rate of growth of sickness absence	From year 1 to 2 there was a growth of 11.1% (10/90x100), and from year 2 to 3 there was a growth rate of 10% (10/100x100)

The manager has undertaken some research and found that certain changes to the rotas, more flexible working, and training have resulted in falls in sickness rates by over 25% in three other nurseries. The manager considers there is a 90% probability that if the same changes are made in this nursery, the impact on sickness rates will be the same. Therefore, using the above statistics, the manager predicts the level of sickness related absence for next year to be a total of 93 days.

This has been calculated by taking the current year's number of days absence (110 days), and adding the estimated growth rate, (so far the average has increased by 10 days per year, hence assume next year's rate to be 120 days), less 90% of 25%, (22.5%) to take account of the effectiveness of the changes that are to be made.

---

120 - 27 (22.5% of 120) = 93 days
divided by 10 staff = 9.3 days per member of staff

If this prediction is correct, the average sickness level per staff member will be 9.3 days, which is 16.25% greater than the target number of 8 days ($\frac{9.3 - 8}{8}$ x 100), a significant improvement on the current year when the average rate was 11 days, 37.5% above the 8 day average ($\frac{11 - 8}{8}$ x 100).

From this information, the manager can give a reasoned estimate of what the expenditure on agency staff should be for next year, as 93 days will need to be covered. If the average daily rate for agency staff is £80 per day, then the manager could justify allocating a budget of £7,440 for agency staff costs, (93 days x £80).

Exercise 3

Consider the following 2 scenarios and indicate which of the central tendency measures are most appropriate. Explain your answer highlighting any potential difficulties you may have with the decision making process.

Scenario A

You have just taken over the management of a refuse collection team with 9 area managers. You wish to set a performance target with respect to the number of bins emptied per hour. You have obtained the following current average rates per hour from each area:

Area	1	2	3	4	5	6	7	8	9
Bins per hour	12	6	10	10	8	10	10	6	10

Most Appropriate Central Tendency Measure (s)

Reason

Potential difficulties with choice

Suggested solution given on page 66.

Scenario B

You have been engaged as a consultant in a crisis management situation. The local authority housing department has hit a crisis point where services have to be drastically cut. You have suggested that at least 4 area offices be closed, based on those attracting the lowest number of monthly users. Using a central tendency measure as a cut off point, justify which offices you would close.

Area	1	2	3	4	5	6	7	8	9
Ave. no. users per month	160	200	220	160	280	230	400	160	440
Region	North	North	West	West	South	South	South	East	East

Most Appropriate Central Tendency Measure (s)

Reason

Potential difficulties with choice

Suggested solution given on page 67.

Exercise 4

Drawing on your own experience, indicate your use of statistics for each of the following areas:

Purpose	How statistics have been (could be) used	Where the data came (could come) from	Potential Improvements
Performance Measurement	*e.g. percentage increase in productivity, such as number of clients seen, number of forms completed, etc.*	*e.g. visitors book, time log, client records, performance indicators etc.*	*e.g. more data collected at first meeting*
Decision Making	*e.g. reduced service demand levels, leading to service closure*	*e.g. general statistics on population growth*	*e.g. more specific data by client type and by area*

Use of statistics continued

Purpose	How statistics have been (could be) used	Where the data came (could come) from	Potential Improvements
Forward Planning	*e.g. estimating probabilities of future events, i.e. potential sickness levels and need for agency staff*	*e.g. historic data on sickness levels and trends in work practice that impact on sickness levels*	*e.g. better systems for data collection and predictions*
Customer Relations	*e.g. customer satisfaction ratings and customer complaints*	*e.g. annual customer survey, complaints register*	*e.g. more frequent and specific survey forms, pro-active complaints policy*
Marketing	*e.g. promoting success, e.g. reduction on rent arrears by x%*	*e.g. service data on performance indicators*	*e.g. coordination of information to identify successes*

Chapter 4

USING SPREADSHEETS

Technological advances have meant that more and more public sector managers have access to computers and software products. Spreadsheets are one of the most popular types of software packages, and can be of considerable assistance when used for numerical and financial analysis. There are a number of spreadsheet packages available in the marketplace, but all have the same basic functions and can be used in a similar way.

Basic Spreadsheet Functions

In the current environment, it is advisable for all staff to acquire a basic level of computer literacy which will enable them to use a spreadsheet. There are many courses available allowing for skills development in this area, and some organisations offer in house training. All spreadsheet packages follow the same basic principles with respect to their operation, and the following diagram sets out the most basic aspects of a spreadsheet.

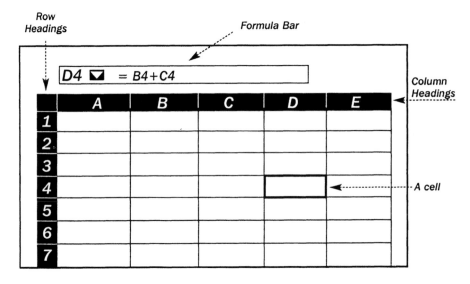

All spreadsheets have formula bars, rows, columns and cells, and these are described as follows:

Formula Bar	This shows the formula that has been entered into a particular cell, and the result of the formula is shown in the cell itself.
Column and Row Headings	Column and Row headings are used to reference cells. Each individual cell will have a unique reference incorporating a letter representing the column and a number representing the row. For example, the highlighted cell on the diagram shows cell reference D4.
Cells	These are where you enter data. This could be text, numbers or formulas. Cells can be formatted to display the data in different ways such as percentages, date, time etc. The information can also be presented in different formats such as bold, underlined, etc.

Why use Spreadsheets

A spreadsheet is a flexible tool which can be used to meet an individual manager's requirements to record, manipulate, analyse and present numerical data. Although these are its primary purpose, some spreadsheets also have other uses such as a database facility. Spreadsheets are relatively user friendly and attending an appropriate course will quickly provide the basics. Spreadsheets take the physical labour out of undertaking repetitive calculations, and given that the formulae are correctly used, the results of the spreadsheet calculations will always be correct. Public sector managers tend to use spreadsheets in the following ways:

a)   **To assist in financial record keeping**

The spreadsheet will allow entries to be made for all financial transactions, in a very similar way to a manual accounting system. Whether this is the most suitable tool for financial record keeping in any given service area, depends on a number of different issues such as the volume of transactions; for example, a large organisation or service area with many transactions may be best served by a fully integrated accounting package containing all the books of account such as a nominal ledger.

b)   **To assist in budget monitoring and control**

Many public sector organisations now operate accounting systems which enable managers to access information. The problem for many managers is information may not be presented in a format suitable for monitoring purposes. In some cases information can be transferred from the accounting system to a spreadsheet (ideally electronically) allowing the manager to modify the presentation and make comparisons with budgets, calculate variances (the difference between budgets and actuals), adjust the actual figures to take account of committed expenditure and so on. The spreadsheet will enable the monitoring information to be designed in a way that best meets the manager's needs. It can also be prepared and printed whenever needed.

c)   **To calculate unit costs**

A spreadsheet can be used to record unit costs. For example, a social services department may wish to know the cost of a client's care package. If individual costs can be attributed to a particular client, this could be recorded and totalled on a spreadsheet. If this is obtained for a number of clients, then the average unit cost per client can be calculated by aggregating all the individual care package costs and dividing by the number of clients.

d)   For financial forecasting
This is perhaps the most common use of the spreadsheet. Most organisations have to prepare forecasts of future income and expenditure, and some forecast cash flows. Once established, the spreadsheet allows for constant change which is necessary when trying to predict the future. The spreadsheet model will also enable the user to enter a range of figures based on differing scenarios, to establish what the future might look like under each scenario.

e)   For financial planning
Having developed financial forecasts, these can then be used for financial planning. The forecast will be based on a number of assumptions, ideally arising from a business plan. When the forecasts are finalised, the organisation will know exactly what level of budget is needed, or whether there are cash flow shortages, etc. Finances can then be planned based on the forecast, for example, an organisation may need to extend its overdraft facilities as part of its financial plan.

f)   To develop tailored financial reports for information and decision-making
Spreadsheets contain a variety of formatting tools which mean reports generated from a spreadsheet package can be tailored for easy reading, expediency, content, relevance etc.

g)   To undertake financial analysis
Formulas can be entered into cells within the spreadsheet, which can assist in calculating percentages, comparatives and projections, these can then be used for financial analysis.

h) To record research data results
The spreadsheet does not only have to be used in a financial context. Data of any kind can be entered onto a spreadsheet for analysis. It may be used to perform functions as simple as sorting the data into relevant categories, date order, ascending/ descending values and so on.

i) To undertake statistical analysis of research data
In the case of numerical data, the spreadsheet can be developed to undertake a wide range of calculations as described in the section 'Using Statistics'. The most common are percentages, growth rates, and comparisons.

j) To develop charts and graphs
A table of data can be entered onto a spreadsheet and used to produce charts and graphs. These tend to be very useful for presentation purposes, and some find a pictorial illustration of results far more understandable than a table of numbers.

Developing Financial Spreadsheets

As previously stated, spreadsheets are particularly useful for forecasting and undertaking financial management and control activities such as variance analysis. Public sector managers should gain an understanding of at least these two uses of the spreadsheet, even if other staff are primarily responsible for these areas.

Ideally, different scenarios can be applied to a forecast and the most likely outcome used as a basis for budget setting. Producing several different forecasts, with varying assumptions, enables the manger to quickly assess the financial implications of each scenario. When the forecast spreadsheet has been developed, assumptions can be easily changed and revised forecasts produced very quickly. Constructing the spreadsheet may be time consuming, however, once an initial template has been developed, it can be copied and used over and over again.

An example of an Income and Expenditure forecast for a Parks service cost centre is shown as follows:

Parks Service	Apr £	May £	Jun £	Jul £	Aug £	Sep £	Oct £	Nov £	Dec £	Jan £	Feb £	Mar £	Total £
Income													
Budget	10,000	10,000	10,000	12,000	12,000	12,000	12,000	12,000	12,000	12,000	12,000	12,000	138,000
Cafe Sales	500	750	800	1,000	800	1,000	1,000	800	500	500	750	800	9,200
Total	10,500	10,750	10,800	13,000	12,800	13,000	13,000	12,800	12,500	12,500	12,750	12,800	147,200
Expenditure													
Employee Costs	9,000	9,000	9,000	9,000	9,000	9,000	9,000	9,000	9,000	9,000	9,000	9,000	108,000
Operational Costs	2,000	2,000	2,000	2,000	2,000	2,000	2,000	2,000	2,000	2,000	2,000	2,000	24,000
Supp't Service Costs	1,000	1,000	1,000	1,000	1,000	1,000	1,000	1,000	1,000	1,000	1000	1000	12,000
Total	12,000	12,000	12,000	12,000	12,000	12,000	12,000	12,000	12,000	12,000	12,000	12,000	144,000
Net Surplus Deficit	-1,500	-1,250	-1,200	1,000	800	1,000	1,000	800	500	500	750	800	3,200

Instead of feeding precise figures into each cell, it may be relevant to use a formula. For example, using the previous Parks Service spreadsheet, if the Café's sales are based on each customer spending an average of £5, and the anticipated number of customers are known for each month, then a spreadsheet can be developed using formulas to calculate the monthly income as follows:

B12 ☑	= (B6*B9)					
	A	**B**	**C**	**D**	**E**	**F**
1	**Estimated Customer Usage**					
2						
3		APR	MAY	JUN	JUL	AUG
4						
5	No. of					
6	customers	100	150	160	200	160
7						
8	Spend per					
9	Customer	5	5	5	5	5
10						
11	Total					
12	Income	500	750	800	1000	800

As shown in the example, the expected number of monthly customers has been entered into cell range B6 to F6, and the expected spend per customer has been entered into cell range B9 to F9. In order to calculate the expected income, we can develop a formula which multiplies the number of customers expected in a given month by the expected spend per customer. These formulas have been entered into the income cell range B12 to F12. As shown in the formula bar, the income for April has been calculated by multiplying the volume of customers from cell B6, by the expected spend per customer from B9. The formula entered into cell B12 is, therefore =(B6*B9). A similar formula has been used to calculate the income for each of the remaining months making reference to the relevant cells. For example, the formula for calculating income for May is =(C6*C9), for June is =(D6*D9), for July is =(E6*E9), and for August is =(F6*F9). A template set up in this way, allows the user to make changes to the assumptions about the volume and expected spend of customers, and have the forecast automatically updated.

This basic spreadsheet could be extended to consider a variety of scenarios, for example:

a) If a marketing campaign was expected to generate an increase of 20% in customer numbers, a formula to calculate the total income for April would be as follows:

B15 ☑ =((B6+(B6*20%))*B9)

	A	B	C	D	E	F
13	Scenario A - 20% increase in number of customers					
14						
15	Total income	600	900	960	1200	960

b) If, on the other hand, a fall in quality standards was expected to lead to a 10% decrease in customer numbers, a formula to calculate the total income for April would be as follows:

B15 ☑ =((B6-(B6*10%))*B9)

	A	B	C	D	E	F
13	Scenario B - 10% decrease in number of customers					
14						
15	Total income	450	675	720	900	720

Similar formulas could be produced to calculate the income and cost implications for all types of scenarios.

Exercise 5

Developing a spreadsheet

Using the following profile information, develop a spreadsheet commencing from the start of the financial year, April, which shows the monthly profile of each area of income and expenditure.

Profile assumptions

1 The main source of income will be a grant of £500,000, which is expected to be received quarterly in advance, the first quarter being in April.

2 Other income will be received during the year as a result of a number of planned fundraising activities. An estimate of £50,000 is expected with 50% of that being raised during August as a result of a festival, and the balance being raised from a Christmas party.

3 A small amount of income will be achieved through sales which cannot be planned for. It is estimated that this will total approximately £6,000 for the year. A straight-line profile should be applied.

4 The main expenditure will be on salaries and it is expected that there will be a stable staff group. However, there is a vacancy for a deputy manager and this will be filled in August, on an annual salary of £36,000 including on-costs. The total budget for salaries including all on-costs is £480,000, which takes account of the new employee's salary from August onwards.

5 There is a direct cost of sales, which represents 50% of the sales value. (See point 3)

6 Overhead costs including accommodation, utilities, etc. need to be paid on a monthly basis and have been based on last years charges of £36,000.

7 Marketing costs, including leaflets, postage, etc. will be incurred as part of the fund-raising activities. These will need to be incurred two months before the fund-raising events and a budget of £10,000 has been allocated for each event.

8 Miscellaneous expenses will be incurred every month, but these will be paid for out of the budget of £9,000. It is expected that twice as much will be spent in the second six months as in the first six months.

Suggested solution on page 68.

Exercise 6

How well are you using your spreadsheet?

Which of the following do you, could you, or should you use a spreadsheet for.

	Do Use √	Could Use √	Should Use √
1. Financial Record Keeping			
2. Budget Monitoring and Control			
3. Calculating Unit Costs			
4. Financial Forecasting			
5. Financial Planning			
6. Financial Reports			
7. Financial Analysis			
8. Research Data Collation			
9. Statistical Analysis			
10. Charts and Graphs			

How could your use of spreadsheets be improved?

Chapter 5

PROJECT APPRAISAL

In an environment where financial resources are limited, project appraisal techniques can be useful in helping a manager to decide how best to utilise those limited resources. Project appraisal techniques provide methods of comparing similar and dis-similar projects in a formal and objective way. This should not, however, detract from the very many issues, some of which are non-financial, which comes into play when making project decisions in a public sector environment.

This chapter will describe the basic calculations required with respect to the following project appraisal techniques:

- **Payback Period**
- **Return on Investment**
- **Net Present Value**
- **Internal Rate of Return**

The above techniques are commonly used in the private sector, particularly in relation to investment decision making. For example, whether or not to borrow money to invest in a project, or when making choices between competing projects.

In the public sector, applying traditional approaches to project appraisal does present difficulties. Some of the typical problems are identified as follows:

- **Many of the projects that require investment do not have easily measurable financial returns**

- The way in which public funds can be used is often restricted by legislation

- There is often a political dimension to decision making, particularly with respect to major projects and hence, the objective approach may be overshadowed by politics and other issues

- The public sector has to be risk averse with public money

- Public sector organisations are restricted by the way in which they can raise funds, and borrowing funds is often not possible

- Due to the nature of public sector funding, many public sector organisations cannot take a very long term view, and hence projects are appraised over a short timeframe, often one year

Given that public sector organisations have a duty to produce the best value for money service, some of the following techniques, if correctly applied, can be very useful for decision making.

Payback Period (PB)

This is one of the simplest methods of assessing potential investments. It basically calculates how quickly the returns arising from the financial investment, "pay back" the total investment. Most people understand this approach in terms of "how quickly will I get my money back?".

For example:

> *If a local authority were to invest £50,000 in new technology which would create annual efficiency savings of £12,500 mainly due to saving staff time, then the payback period would be 4 years. This is calculated by dividing the sum invested, by the annual return generated (in this case savings).*

$$\frac{Sum\ Invested}{Annual\ Return} \quad = \quad \frac{£50,000}{£12,500} \quad = 4\ years$$

If the annual saving achieved was £20,000, then the payback period would only be 2½ years.

In this example, deciding whether or not to invest the £50,000 would depend on the following:

- *The importance attached to generating a return or saving on the investment?*

- *What targets exist for the length of the pay back period?*

- *Are there any alternative projects that the £50,000 could be spent on?*

- *Does the £50,000 have to be borrowed and what is the cost of that borrowing?*

- *What, if any, other non financial costs/savings are associated with the investment?*

If an alternative project was available to the local authority, such as investing in security systems, where the payback on the £50,000 was only £5,000 per annum, then the payback period would be 10 years. Common sense would lead most people to choose the first project which showed a payback period of 4 years because it was the quickest. However, this is not always the correct decision. For example:

In the case of the investment in technology, it could be assumed that the savings generated would only last for 5 years as after this time the technology may have become obsolete and further investment would be required. The total savings would, therefore, be £62,500. (i.e. 5 x £12,500)

> *In the case of the security systems, it could be assumed the system would have a useful life of 15 years, and hence make continued savings of £5,000 per annum during that time. The total savings would then be £75,000 (i.e. 15 x £5,000)*
>
> *If it were possible to take a long term view, then the project with the longer payback period presents a larger long term saving, and hence a decision could sway in favour of this project.*

There are strong arguments for deciding on projects with the shortest payback period because of the time value of money, and the fact that money today is worth more than money tomorrow. We discuss how to calculate the time value of money in the section covering Net Present Value (NPV).

Return on Investment (ROI)

This ratio is often used by companies as a measure of performance. It tells shareholders the level of "return" they are achieving from their investment in the business. They can then compare this with the return they could be achieving elsewhere, for example, in an alternative investment or on a deposit account. Ideally, they would expect a better return if they are taking a greater risk. The ROI is used in a similar way to appraise projects.

In order to calculate the ROI, the average annual return of the project is divided by the projects capital outlay and multiplied by 100 to obtain a percentage.

$$\frac{\text{Average Annual Return}}{\text{Capital Outlay}} \text{ x 100}$$

When presented as a percentage, the ROI can then be compared with other projects or alternative uses of the capital. The ROI can also be used as a benchmark, where an organisation may also have a minimum return on investment which all projects have to achieve in order to be considered for investment.

In the public sector, the definition of return may not be profit, it may be one or a combination of factors which need to be expressed in financial terms and include the following:

- **Savings**
- **Waste Reduction**
- **Prevention**
- **Increased efficiency**
- **Increased customer satisfaction**
- **Reduced complaints**
- **Reduced staff turnover**
- **Improved safety, etc.**

An example of how ROI can be calculated in a public sector environment is shown as follows:

Which Project?

Council Members are deciding how they can allocate reserves that have been accumulated in the General Fund to worthwhile community projects. In the light of Best Value they intend to use ROI as the criteria for potential investment. The current ruling interest rates for funds on deposit are 5%. The amount available for the capital outlay is £600,000 and the two most popular project ideas have been selected for appraisal.

Project 1
A recycling plant that will last for 10 years. The savings will be equivalent to £50,000 for the first 5 years and £70,000 thereafter, however, there is a working capital cost with respect to running the plant of £10,000 per year.

Project 2
A leisure centre development with an expected life of 7 years before major works are required. The expected income generation is £400,000 per annum with running costs of £340,000.

Project 1 ROI
Average annual net savings

$$\frac{(50,000 \times 5) + (70,000 \times 5) - (10,000 \times 10)}{10} = £50,000$$

$$ROI \quad \frac{Average\ Net\ Savings}{Capital\ Outlay} \quad \frac{50,000}{600,000} \times 100 \quad = 8.33\%$$

Project 2 ROI
Average annual net profit $400,000 - 340,000$ $= £60,000$

$$ROI \quad \frac{Average\ Net\ Profit}{Capital\ Outlay} \quad \frac{60,000}{600,000} \times 100 \quad = 10.00\%$$

Both projects have a ROI which is greater than the interest rate that would be earned if the funds were placed on deposit. If the projects are mutually exclusive, i.e. only one project can be undertaken, then using the ROI for decision making would result in project 2 being selected.

Although in this example project 2 is selected there are some issues that have not been taken into account:

- *Project 1 has a longer life and hence, the total savings of £500,000 (10 years x £50,000) are greater than the total profit £420,000 (7 years x £60,000) to be earned from project 2*
- *As with the payback method, no account has been taken of the time value of money*

Ideally these two factors should be taken into account when making a final decision.

Net Present Value (NPV)

This technique enables managers to appraise projects whilst taking account of the time value of money. The method assumes that due to inflation, money today is worth more than money tomorrow. It then calculates future income at today's values by using a discount rate. This is best explained by considering the following:

If today someone invested £100 at an interest rate of 6%, then at the end of year 1, the £100 would be worth £106 (100 + 6% of 100). If that money continued to be invested for a second year, it would be worth £112.36 (106 + 6% of 106), and so on. This process is referred to as "compound interest", and tables which assist in its calculation can be found on page 71. NPV is the reverse of this approach. In order to calculate what £100 would be worth in one or more years' time, it has to be discounted by a discount factor based on the discount rate selected. The mathematical tables showing the discount factors for the net present value of money, can be found on page 71.

Assuming a discount rate of 6%, the discount factor for 1 year in the future, is 0.9434 (see table), which means that £100 in a year's time will only be worth £94.34 in today's money. (This can be checked by increasing £94.34 by 6% which is equal to £100).

The NPV calculation can have a dramatic effect on decision making with respect to project appraisal, because a project which looked viable may become unviable when the future returns are stated at present values. Consider the following example:

The manager of a residential home has, through fund-raising, managed to acquire £10,000 to invest in a small project. The manager has been given permission to spend this money on any project as long as the £10,000 is recovered after five years through savings. The project under consideration is the purchase of a second hand mini van which would save hire charges, and also mean an improvement in the quality of service to the residents as they would be able to go out more often and not be limited to time constraints. The van is expected to last for 5 years and the annual saving is expected to average £2,000. The manager considers this to be a good use of funds as the savings, when adjusted for inflation at 2% per annum for hire charges, will be greater than the initial cash outlay.

Using the tables on page 71 showing the future value of money, the manager has calculated the following using a rate of 2%:

Year	Saving	Rate 2%	Future value
1	2,000	1.0200	2,040
2	2,000	1.0404	2,081
3	2,000	1.0612	2,122
4	2,000	1.0824	2,165
5	2,000	1.1041	2,208
Total	£10,000		£10,616

The manager presented this analysis to the senior management board stating that over the 5 years there would be a £10,616 saving, which is in excess of the initial cash

---

outlay. However, the finance manager said this would not be the case if the time value of money was taken into account. Given that ruling interest rates were 6%, the finance manager suggested that the savings should be discounted at this rate to give the real value of the savings in today's money. The manager was asked to re-calculate his figures on this basis.

Using the present value tables on page 71, the following figures were produced:

Year	Saving including inflation	Discount Rate 6%	Present value
1	2,040	.9434	1,924
2	2,081	.8900	1,852
3	2,122	.8396	1,782
4	2,165	.7621	1,650
5	2,208	.7473	1,650
Total	£10,616		£8,858

By taking into account the time value of money, it shows that the savings at today's value are now only £8,858 falling short of the initial cash outlay of £10,000.

If it was critical that the savings had to be equal or more than the initial cash outlay after five years, instead of deciding to go ahead with the project, the manager would have to select another project with greater savings. However, the manager may still argue strongly to go ahead with the project as long as other benefits relating to service quality can be justified.

As shown from this example, net present values do assist in decision making by taking future savings, returns, income, etc and discounting them to reflect present values so more accurate comparisons can be made. Again there are a number of issues that need to be taken into account when using this technique:

- *The discount rate used - it usually reflects the ruling interest rates of the day as this would be the minimum that could be achieved if the funds were placed on deposit*
- *The way in which returns, or savings arise. The real benefit arising from some projects are in the long term and not the short term*
- *There is an assumption that rates will be constant over time, e.g. the inflation rate and interest rate*

Internal Rate of Return (IRR)

The internal rate of return is the discount rate that equates the value of expected future cash inflows, savings, returns, etc. to the initial outlay. Using the earlier mini-van example, this would be the rate which would equate the savings from investing in the mini-van, to the initial cost, that is £10,000.

The simplest way to calculate the IRR is through trial and error. This involves undertaking a number of NPV calculations at different rates until the rate at which the present value equals the initial cash outlay is found. This process can be performed either by using a scientific calculator which has this function, or on a spreadsheet whereby the appropriate formulas can be set up and then easily changed.

Exercise 7

The Head Teacher of Midbank School has been offered £100,000 by a local technology firm to invest in a technology related project. The Head's task is to maximise the income generated over the life of the project, to assist in contributing to the schools annual revenue expenditure. The Head is currently considering two potential projects, and has decided to use standard project appraisal techniques as a starting point for a report recommending one or other of the projects to the Board of Governors.

The two projects are described as follows:

Learning on Line

- The set up costs of this web site will be £100,000
- Income will be generated through annual subscriptions, and are expected to grow substantially year on year as more and more people have access to and use the Internet
- Annual costs will be very low as information will be generated internally and website maintenance will be undertaken by one of the teachers
- The net subscription income over five years is estimated as follows:

Year	Income (£)
1	10,000
2	20,000
3	30,000
4	40,000
5	50,000

Cybercafe

- The set up costs of the venue will be £100,000.
- Income will be generated through Internet use, sales of food and drinks.
- The net sales income is expected to decrease over the years as more competition comes into the market, however, there is currently no competition and large net revenues are expected in the early years
- The net income over five years is estimated as follows:

Year	Income (£)
1	40,000
2	35,000
3	30,000
4	25,000
5	20,000

Given the above information, appraise the two projects over a 5 year period using the ROI and payback methods, and make recommendations as to which project should be undertaken.

Assuming a 5% interest rate, if adjustments are made for the present value of money, would this change your decision?

Suggested solutions are on page 69.

Chapter 6

PRESENTING FINANCIAL INFORMATION

Financial information can be open to numerous interpretations, all of which can be factually correct, and hence presentation is critical when making a case for gaining grants, acquiring investments, bidding for larger budgets, justifying overspends and so on.

Financial information is often presented using either tables, graphs, or charts. Whichever method is used, the following points are important:

- It should be accurate in every way, for example totals must agree and calculations must be correct
- It should be complete and up to date; the financial information will not be useful if a large part is missing. For example, a manager presents a report that should cover April to June, if June's figures are not available, the report becomes invalid
- It should be easy to read, which means a simple layout where the figures are not too small or close together and the key numbers, such as totals, are highlighted
- It should be "relevant" information with respect to the case being made
- All the figures presented should be supported by detailed written assumptions which are easily cross-referred

As stated in Chapter 4, Using Spreadsheets, the spreadsheet is one of the most useful tools with which to manipulate financial information. It can be used to develop tables or produce graphs and charts. The spreadsheet also enables formulas to be used, which can easily be changed along with the financial data itself.

Using Tables

A table is described in the dictionary as a set of facts or figures systematically displayed in columns and rows. Tables are ideal for financial information, however, before preparing any table, the manager should consider the following:

• The headings for the rows and columns such that the information can be easily understood
• The type of calculations to be undertaken - complex ones will need to be explained
• The sign convention with respect to positive and negative figures; for negative figures, the norm is to use a minus sign (-) or to show the negative figures in brackets.
• Where to use totals and sub totals, and how to make them stand out
• The assumptions being made with respect to the financial information being displayed

Consider the following example:

> *A manager responsible for three one stop shops is required to analyse and interpret their financial performance in the first 4 months of operation, and to present a financial report to the management board.*
>
> *The monthly expenditure information opposite has been supplied by the three shops:*

	Shop A £	Shop B £	Shop C £	Total £
April	35,000	10,000	3,000	48,000
May	55,000	25,000	25,000	105,000
June	15,000	38,000	40,000	93,000
July	20,000	42,000	42,000	104,000
Total	**125,000**	**115,000**	**110,000**	**350,000**

The initial annual budget for the three one stop shops was £1,020,000, which was based purely on estimates and guess work. The manager now wishes to make a number of points and recommendations as a result of the financial analysis undertaken including making a case for increasing the budget; having operated the service for four months, it would seem that at the current rate of expenditure, the total budget will be exceeded. The financial information package the manager is to prepare will include the following:

- *A budget variance analysis*
- *The projected outturn*
- *A unit cost per enquiry at each shop*

The manager considers the most effective presentation will be to use tables.

Using the one stop shop example, several tables are shown on the following pages which illustrate the presentation of the financial information.

A budget variance analysis

This report shows the variance between year to date spend and the budget. It also identifies the balance of the total budget.

Assumptions made:

- Budget is profiled on a straight line basis, that is, equally over 12 months
- Actual expenditure includes creditors (goods and services used for which invoices have yet to be paid)
- Unfavourable variances are stated as negative figures (-)

Cost Centre: One Stop Shops   **Period ended 31 July 2000**

	Total Budget	*Profiled Budget to date	Actual Expenditure to date	Variance to date	Variance %	Budget Remaining	Budget Remaining %
	a	b	c	d (b-c)	e ($\frac{d}{b}$x100)	f (a-c)	g ($\frac{f}{a}$x100)
Shop A	360,000	120,000	125,000	-5,000	-4.2	235,000	65.3
Shop B	360,000	120,000	115,000	5,000	4.2	245,000	68.0
Shop C	300,000	100,000	110,000	-10,000	-10.0	190,000	63.3
Total	1,020,000	340,000	350,000	-10,000	-2.9	670,000	65.7

* calculated by taking 4/12 of the total budget.

Analysis

The period of time under consideration represents one third of the year, and is therefore a good time to review performance. There is a small overspend by shop A, but the monthly figures appear to show that May was an exceptionally high month which may have distorted the figures. Conversely shop B shows a small under spend, but with increasing expenditure in June and July. Shop C shows a larger overspend and increasing expenditure month on month. There is an overall overspend on the cost centre with less than two thirds of the budget remaining for the rest of the year.

The projected outturn

Given the above budget variance analysis, it is clearly important to project the outturn.

Assumptions made:

* Future expenditure will continue at the same rate as expenditure in the first 4 months.

Cost Centre: One Stop Shops **Period ended 31 July 2000**

	Actual Expenditure to date	*Projected outturn	Original Budget	Projected Year end variance	**Variance %	Action To be Taken
Shop A	125,000	375,000	360,000	-15,000	-4.2	Potential for virement
Shop B	115,000	345,000	360,000	15,000	4.2	Potential for virement
Shop C	110,000	330,000	300,000	-30,000	-10.0	Need additional resources
Total	**350,000**	**1,050,000**	**1,020,000**	**-30,000**	**-2.9**	

*   calculated by dividing Actual Expenditure to date by 4 and multiplying by 12.

** calculated by dividing projected year end variance by the original budget and multiplying by 100.

Analysis

Clearly, there is a projected overspend for the end of year position, which should ideally be corrected by implementing the actions identified.

A unit cost per enquiry at each shop

Assumptions made:

- Enquiries have been counted by each shop accurately and completely
- Best Value team have a benchmark unit cost per enquiry for each one stop shop, which will act as the performance standard

Cost Centre: One Stop Shops   **Period ended 31 July 2000**

	No of Enquiries to date	Actual Expenditure to date	*Cost per Enquiry	Best Value Benchmark Unit Cost	Variance
Shop A	4,000	125,000	31.25	30.00	-1.25
Shop B	3,100	115,000	37.10	30.00	-7.10
Shop C	3,700	110,000	29.72	30.00	0.28
Total	**10,800**	**350,000**	**32.41**	**30.00**	**-2.41**

*Actual Expenditure divided by number of enquiries

Analysis

Shop A is nearly hitting the benchmark target, although there is a small overspend. Shop B has a considerably higher unit cost than the benchmark and is under spending on the budget. Both indicate that the volume of throughput is low relative to the other shop. Shop C is hitting the unit cost target even though there is an overspend on the budget. This indicates that the shop is working efficiently but is under resourced. Hence, as pointed out by the projected outturn table, a request for additional funds for Shop C could be justified.

Using Graphs and Charts

It is often more effective to present numerical information in the form of a graph because it gives an immediate visual impact, particularly if it relates to trends and comparisons. The most typical forms of graphs are shown as follows:

Bar Graph

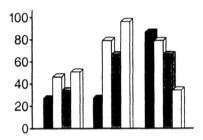

Line Graph

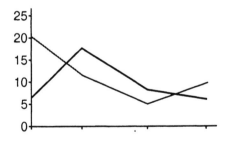

Pie Chart

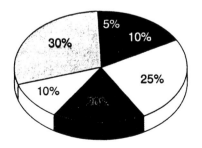

The type of graph used can be extremely influential as to how information is interpreted. We discuss bar graphs, line graphs and pie charts below.

Bar Graph (Histograms)

The bar graph displays frequency distribution and is one of the most useful visual displays of information. The chart has two axes labelled x and y, which usually measure frequency against a variable. Using the One Stop Shop example, we could plot a bar chart showing the level of monthly expenditure for shop A. The months are displayed on the x axis, and the level of expenditure (frequency) are represented on the y axis. This clearly shows which months have the highest expenditure levels.

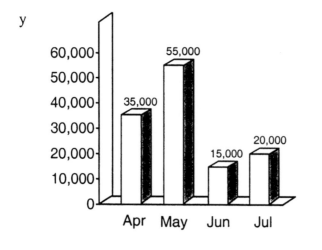

Line Graph (frequency polygons)

The results plotted on the bar graph can be changed to points, and a line drawn linking each of the points. This kind of representation is particularly useful when comparing results. For example, comparing data for the same activity for different years, would establish if a trend existed year on year. Line graphs are particularly effective if a number of different data sets relating to the same topic need to be represented at the same time. Using the One Stop Shop example, the following line graph shows the monthly expenditure for each of the three shops, and an immediate comparison can be made of monthly spending patterns.

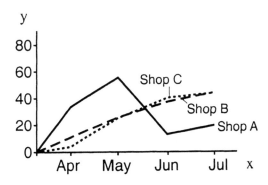

Pie Chart

A pie chart is particularly effective in showing the proportionate distribution of data amongst a group or range of activities. Continuing with the One Stop Shop example, it would be possible to show the proportionate use of different types of service that represent the shop's activities: For example:

General Advice and Information	25%
Housing Enquiries	20%
Planning Enquiries	10%
Social Service Enquiries	30%
Legal Enquiries	5%
Other	10%

This shows more clearly how the demand levels are split between different types of service.

Based on the proportional use of services, a pie chart could be created as follows.

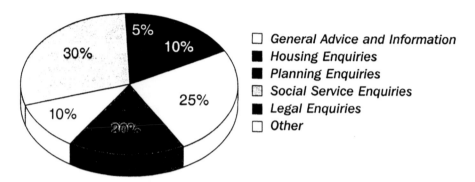

☐ *General Advice and Information*
■ *Housing Enquiries*
■ *Planning Enquiries*
▨ *Social Service Enquiries*
■ *Legal Enquiries*
☐ *Other*

All the above graphs and charts are easily prepared using a spreadsheet package. There is usually a charting function that will guide the user through the process of developing a chart and will offer a wide range of different charts to choose from. A manager will then have to decide which chart gives the most effective representation of the numerical and/or financial information being presented.

Solutions to Exercises

Exercise 1

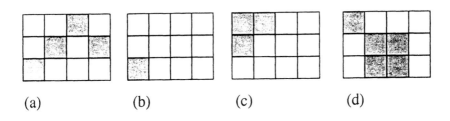

(a)   (b)   (c)   (d)

The fractions in relation to (a), (b), (c), and (d) above are:

(a) 1/3   (b) 1/12   (c) 1/4   (d) 5/12

The fractions in (a), (b), (c) and (d) can be restated as percentages as:

(a) 33.3%   (b) 8.3%   (c) 25%   (d) 41.7%

Exercise 3

Scenario A

First calculate the mean, median, and mode to identify whether or not there is a difference in the central tendency.

Mean	82/9 = 9.1
Median (central number)	10
Mode	10

The most appropriate measure is the mode, which happens to be the same value as the median.

The reason that 10 would be the best target is because:

- This is a standard which most areas seem to be able to meet on average, and therefore it is not unfair to expect all areas to reach this as a minimum
- It is higher than the mean, and as most areas are reaching levels above the mean, this target will not be sufficiently challenging.

The main difficulty is that by setting this as the standard it may demotivate the areas that are already achieving a greater level than this, hence providing no incentive to improve.

Also it does not take regional differences into account. Some houses may be closer together than others, hence facilitating speedier collection.

Scenario B

First calculate the mean, median, and mode to identify whether or not there is a difference in the central tendency.

Mean	2250/9 = 250
Median (central number)	220
Mode	160

The most appropriate measure is the median, which is the middle value of the data series.

• The reason that 220 is a good cut off point, is that as the middle value, there are 4 offices with lower monthly users and 4 with higher monthly users. A case can be made for closing the offices with the 4 lowest numbers of monthly users.

The main difficulty in making this decision, is that it does not take account of the regional locations of the office. This may result in some regions not having an office at all, which would be an even worse service for the users and perhaps politically unacceptable.

Exercise 5

	Apr £	May £	Jun £	Jul £	Aug £	Sep £	Oct £	Nov £	Dec £	Jan £	Feb £	Mar £	Total £
Income													
Grant	125,000			125,000			125,000			125,000			500,000
Fund Raising					25,000				25,000				50,000
Sales	500	500	500	500	500	500	500	500	500	500	500	500	6,000
Total	125,500	500	500	125,500	25,500	500	125,500	500	25,500	125,500	500	500	556,000
Expenditure													
Salaries	*38,000	38,000	38,000	38,000	41,000	41,000	41,000	41,000	41,000	41,000	41,000	41,000	480,000
Cost of Sales	250	250	250	250	250	250	250	250	250	250	250	250	3,000
Overhead costs	3,000	3,000	3,000	3,000	3,000	3,000	3,000	3,000	3,000	3,000	3,000	3,000	36,000
Marketing			10,000				10,000						20,000
Miscellaneous	500	500	500	500	500	500	1,000	1,000	1,000	1,000	1,000	1,000	9,000
Total	41,750	41,750	51,750	41,750	44,750	44,750	55,250	45,250	45,250	45,250	45,250	45,250	548,000
Net Surplus Deficit	83,750	-41,250	-51,250	83,750	-19,250	-44,250	70,250	-44,750	-19,750	80,250	-44,750	-44,750	8,000

* Note, only 8 months of the Deputy Manager's £36,000 salary will be reflected in the year's total salary (i.e $^{8}/_{12}$ x 36,000 = 24,000). Therefore, salary April to July is (£480,000 - £24,000) / 12 = £38,000 per month.

Exercise 7

Learning on Line   Cyber Café

ROI

Average annual net income £30,000*		Average annual net income £30,000*	
Investment	£100,000	Investment	£100,000
ROl	30%		30%

* Total income divided by number of years (£150,000 / 5)

Payback

	Income	Cumulative Income		Income	Cumulative Income
Year 1	10,000	10,000	Year 1	40,000	40,000
2	20,000	30,000	2	35,000	75,000
3	30,000	60,000	3	30,000	105,000
4	40,000	100,000	4	25,000	130,000
5	50,000	150,000	5	20,000	150,000

The pay back period is when £100,000 is recovered, and therefore Learning on line has a payback period of 4 years and Cyber Café 3 Years.

> **Given that the ROI is the same for both projects, the Cyber Café appears to present the quickest payback period and should therefore be selected.**

The above figures can be adjusted for the time value of money using a net present value calculation with a discount factor of 5%.

	Learning on Line				**Cyber Café**		
Year		5% discount factor	NPV			5% discount factor	NPV
1	10,000	.9524	9,524		40,000	.9524	38,096
2	20,000	.9070	18,140		35,000	.9070	31,745
3	30,000	.8638	25,914		30,000	.8638	25,914
4	40,000	.8227	32,908		25,000	.8227	20,567
5	50,000	.7835	39,175		20,000	.7835	15,670
Total	150,000		125,661		150,000		131,992

Adjusting the figures using present values, confirms that the Cyber Café has the highest NPV and should be the chosen project.

The above techniques do not take into account either projects' longer term potential. Learning on Line has growing future income streams, whereas the Cyber Café has declining income streams.

The Cyber Café would appear less risky as income streams are higher in the early years and the accuracy of forecasting tends to diminish over time.

In light of the above, the manager may wish to add some subjective analysis as part of the over all project appraisal process.

Mathematical Tables

Present Value of £1 at the end of (n) periods

Rate / Period	1%	2%	3%	4%	5%	6%	7%	8%	9%	10%
1	.9901	.9804	.9709	.9615	.9524	.9434	.9346	.9259	.9174	.9091
2	.9803	.9612	.9426	.9246	.9070	.8900	.8734	.8573	.8417	.8264
3	.9706	.9423	.9151	.8890	.8638	.8396	.8163	.7938	.7722	.7513
4	.9610	.9238	.8885	.8548	.8227	.7621	.7629	.7350	.7084	.6830
5	.9515	.9057	.8626	.8219	.7835	.7473	.7130	.6806	.6499	.6209
6	.9420	.8880	.8375	.7903	.7462	.7050	.6663	.6302	.5963	.5645
7	.9327	.8706	.8131	.7599	.7107	.6651	.6227	.5835	.5470	.5132
8	.9235	.8535	.7894	.7307	.6768	.6274	.5820	.5403	.5019	.4665
9	.9143	.8368	.7664	.7026	.6446	.5919	.5439	.5002	.4604	.4241
10	.9053	.8203	.7441	.6756	.6139	.5584	.5083	.4632	.4224	.3855
11	.8693	.8043	.7224	.6496	.5847	.5268	.4751	.4289	.3875	.3505
12	.8874	.7885	.7014	.6246	.5568	.4970	.4440	.3971	.3555	.3186
13	.8787	.7730	.6810	.6006	.5303	.4688	.4150	.3677	.3262	.2897
14	.8700	.7579	.6611	.5775	.5051	.4423	.3878	.3405	.2992	.2633
15	.8613	.7430	.6419	.5553	.4810	.4173	.3624	.3152	.2745	.2394

Future Value of £1 at the end of (n) periods (Compound Interest)

Rate / Period	1%	2%	3%	4%	5%	6%	7%	8%	9%	10%
1	1.0100	1.0200	1.0300	1.0400	1.0500	1.0600	1.0700	1.0800	1.0900	1.1000
2	1.0201	1.0404	1.0609	1.0816	1.1025	1.1236	1.1449	1.1664	1.1881	1.2100
3	1.0303	1.0612	1.0927	1.1249	1.1576	1.1910	1.2250	1.2597	1.2950	1.3310
4	1.0406	1.0824	1.1255	1.1699	1.2155	1.2625	1.3108	1.3605	1.4116	1.4641
5	1.0510	1.1041	1.1593	1.2167	1.2763	1.3382	1.4026	1.4693	1.5386	1.6105
6	1.0615	1.1262	1.1941	1.2653	1.3401	1.4185	1.5007	1.5869	1.6771	1.7716
7	1.0721	1.1487	1.2299	1.3159	1.4071	1.5036	1.6058	1.7138	1.8280	1.9487
8	1.0829	1.1717	1.2668	1.3686	1.4775	1.5938	1.7182	1.8509	1.9926	2.1436
9	1.0937	1.1951	1.3048	1.4233	1.5513	1.6895	1.8385	1.9990	2.1719	2.3579
10	1.1046	1.2190	1.3439	1.4802	1.6289	1.7908	1.9672	2.1589	2.3674	2.5937
11	1.1157	1.2434	1.3842	1.5395	1.7103	1.8983	2.1049	2.3316	2.5804	2.8531
12	1.1268	1.2682	1.4258	1.1610	1.7959	2.0122	2.2522	2.5182	2.8127	3.1384
13	1.1381	1.2936	1.4685	1.6651	1.8856	2.1329	2.4098	2.7196	3.0658	3.4523
14	1.1495	1.3195	1.5126	1.7317	1.9799	2.2609	2.5785	2.9372	3.3427	3.7975
15	1.1610	1.3459	1.5580	1.8009	2.0789	2.3966	2.7590	3.1722	3.6425	4.1772

Index